# A True Likeness

# A TRUE LIKENESS

The Black South of
Richard Samuel Roberts
1920-1936

Edited by
Thomas L. Johnson
and
Phillip C. Dunn

Bruccoli Clark
Columbia, S.C.
and
Algonquin Books of Chapel Hill
Chapel Hill, N.C.

Library of Congress Cataloging-in-Publication Data

Roberts, Richard Samuel, d. 1936-
A true likeness.

     1. Photography—South Carolina—Columbia—Por-
traits. 2. Afro-Americans—South Carolina—Columbia
—Social conditions—Pictorial works. 3. Roberts, Richard
Samuel, d. 1936. 4. Afro-American photographers—South
        Carolina—Columbia—Biography. 5. Columbia
(S.C.)—History—Pictorial works. I. Johnson, Thomas L.,
    1935- . II. Dunn, Phillip C., 1947- . III. Title.
      TR680.R63 1986 779'.930555 86-14089
             ISBN 0-912697-48-2 (cloth)
             ISBN 0-912697-47-4 (lim. ed.)
             ISBN 0-912697-50-4 (paper)

For Our Families

Roberts
Johnson
Dunn

# Richard Samuel Roberts: An Introduction
## by Thomas L. Johnson

During the 1920s and 1930s in Columbia, South Carolina, a black man named Richard Samuel Roberts was employed weekdays from four A.M. to noon as a custodian at the U.S. Post Office. When his workday there was done he went a few blocks south to 1119 Washington Street, in the heart of the segregated city's black commercial district, where on the second floor he maintained a photography studio. His clientele was largely the black population of the city. He also often took his equipment to residences, schools, and funeral homes in and around the city and at times he went on picture-taking trips to other cities and towns in the state, as well as into the rural sections.

He had taught himself photography in Fernandina, Florida, while working with his father as a stevedore and later as a fireman-laborer at the post office there. In Fernandina he eventually established and operated The Gem Studio. His wife, Wilhelmina Pearl Selena Williams, was a native of Columbia, and in 1920, after her health had begun to suffer from the humid Florida climate, the Robertses moved to Columbia. They bought a house, and by 1922 Roberts had rented the studio on Washington Street.

He operated his business for close to fifteen years. After his death in 1936 at least a portion of the negatives that Roberts had accumulated over the years—some three thousand glass plates (out of a possible ten thousand pictures he may have made during the Columbia years)—were stored in the crawl space beneath the family home at 1717 Wayne Street.

For almost half a century they remained there—a priceless cache documenting the black community of Columbia and South Carolina during the decades between the two world wars. His children cherished their father's work and at one time had begun retrieving some of the negatives with the hope of having a book of their father's work privately published. But their various career commitments, largely away from Columbia, and the task of removing and transporting the huge number of glass plates—not to mention the complexities of arranging for publication itself—prevented them from bringing such plans to fruition. Thus it was not until 1977 that the chain of events began which led to the public rediscovery of Roberts's work.

That rediscovery came about through the field archival program of the South Caroliniana Library, a research institution that is part of the library system of the University of South Carolina in Columbia. One of the Library's contacts in the black community during the 1970s was Miss Harriett M. Cornwell, a retired schoolteacher living in the city's Arsenal Hill section. Miss Cornwell mentioned that for many years a photographer named Roberts and his family had been her next-door neighbors. One of the four surviving Roberts children still lived there, she said. An initial visit to 1717 Wayne Street established communication not only with Cornelius C. Roberts and his wife Carrie but with the other children of Richard Samuel Roberts: Gerald Emerson Roberts, a government librarian in Washington, D.C.; Beverly Nash Roberts, a retired educator living in Jamaica, New York; and Wilhelmina Roberts Wynn, a retired social worker and educator residing in New York City.

The high quality of the pictures in the hands of the Roberts children was immediately evident. Despite the physical condition of the pictures, all of which were more than forty years old, their clarity, their meticulous but natural composition, and the dignity of the subjects were readily apparent. More exciting was the revelation by the children that much of their father's work survived in the form of the thousands of glass negatives stacked beneath the house. But the condition of the negatives was unknown.

The family generously agreed to talk about their father and his work, and taped interviews were conducted in order to begin assembling at least an oral record of R. S. Roberts's life, his experience as a photographer, and his role as family head in the Roberts households in Florida and South Carolina. The main consideration soon came to be the matter of retrieving the mass of glass negatives from under the house and, if possible, making contact prints from the salvageable ones. The problem was to find a local photographer to do the work, someone who combined technical expertise with an interest in historical photography.

In March 1982, a few of the glass plates were placed in the hands of Phillip C. Dunn, a University of South Carolina art professor whose specialty was photography. Dunn had been shown some of Roberts's photographs; he expressed an interest in the project and said he would like to work with the negatives. His prints of this initial batch of negatives indicated that, miraculously, the plates had survived in excellent condition and made striking images. The sharp, clear pictures were aesthetically pleasing and historically revealing. Here were photographs the likes of which few whites had ever seen or thought existed, and which most of the black community itself either did not know about or had long forgotten.

The Roberts family accepted Dunn's offer to work with the rest of the negatives and approved his role, along with that of the South Caroliniana Library, in the shaping of plans for the permanent preservation of their father's work and its presentation to the public. The task would be a formidable one, involving not only the retrieval and cleaning of the thousands of negatives but also the imposition of archival order upon them, the making of work prints, and identification of the photographic images themselves.

Dunn spent the next two and a half years cleaning and restoring the plates—removing the mildew and termite tracks—and establishing a system of archival preservation and retrieval for the collection. He also made the master set of contact prints from the thousands of negatives that remained in good condition. Together with the Library's field archivist, he isolated 350 of the most powerful and significant photographs and made exhibit-quality prints of them. From these, some 200 would be chosen for public display. For the Columbia Museum had committed itself to mounting a Roberts show to run at the end of 1986, as part of its celebration of Columbia's Bicentennial; and Bruccoli Clark Publishers had taken an option to publish a volume of the photographs, to appear that fall.

The other essential part of the process of rediscovering the work and world of R. S. Roberts has been the effort to identify the subjects of his photographs. Since few of the photographer's studio records turned up, the principal way to begin to find out who or what was portrayed in the collection was to go to survivors from the 1920s and 1930s or to their descendants. The project thus engaged another group of persons without whose help neither book nor exhibit—nor, indeed, any long-range research value of the collection itself—could ever have been achieved: dozens of black Carolinians who collectively spent hundreds of hours poring over the large sheets of contact prints in an attempt to put names with faces and places. Such identifications as have been made are the result of countless informal sessions held in numerous homes in Columbia and other communities around the state. Exciting things happened during these meetings: persons recognized themselves as children; they discovered their parents, brothers, or sisters in portraits which they had never seen or hadn't seen in fifty or sixty years. Hundreds of long-lost relatives, friends, or acquaintances were recognized. Many of the locally famous—and a few of the infamous—were remembered and named. Sometimes those interested in helping to identify the subjects in the pictures came to see them at the South Caroliniana Library, whose field archival program was in charge of the task. In this project, time was of the essence: if the effort to identify people and places in the photos had been delayed further, the main opportunity to do so would have been lost forever. Some of those who were important in the project of identification have since died.

The city to which Richard S. Roberts brought his wife and four children in the spring of 1920 existed as an enigma and a contradiction at heart. With a population of 37,524, Columbia was more an overgrown country town than an urban center. And yet, as the capital of South Carolina, as the seat of its university, and as a trading and distribution hub, it pulsed with the essential business of a state that in the 1920s was still basically rural, ranking "at or near the bottom of the nation in every index of social and economic well-being," as I. A. Newby has pointed out in *Black Carolinians: A History of Blacks in South Carolina from 1895 to 1968* (Columbia: University of South Carolina Press, 1973).

South Carolina-born black educator and journalist Kelly Miller noted in the December 1925 issue of the *New York Messenger* that Columbia was one of two centers in South Carolina where blacks were regarded as more than passive instruments of production (Charleston being the other). With a population of 14,455 blacks in 1920, Negroes comprised 38.5 percent of the city's inhabitants. A decade later the black population was 19,519.

For more than one-third of the city's population, life was a matter of social and legal discrimination, political disfranchisement, and institutionalized public insult. Black Columbians could not live in certain sections of town, could not attend their state university, were denied access to all library, playground, and other public recreational facilities. Scant attention was paid to their needs, interests, or accomplishments in the daily newspapers; but whenever a Negro was apprehended in any form of criminal conduct, he was always identified by race in those dailies. Blacks were not permitted to walk in certain areas of the university or state house grounds; black schoolteachers were paid less than white ones, and many black professionals had to double as skilled or semiskilled laborers or shopkeepers in order to make a living. The uneducated were relegated for the most part to the menial, secondary, subservient jobs. When Richard Roberts's name first appears in *Walsh's Columbia City Directory*, in 1920, it is found at the back of the book in the "Colored Dept." (a category that in Columbia lasted through the 1940s). He is listed as a janitor with the post office.

In addition to being a government center, with a history of interracial struggle for political power following the Civil War, Columbia was also a military town, with Camp Jackson serving as one of the nation's major army training bases during World War I. But black soldiers returning to Columbia from having helped to fight "the war to make the world safe for democracy" found a stronger resolve than ever on the part of the whites to maintain the racial status quo. There were five lynchings in South Carolina in 1921, the year after Roberts moved to Columbia and about the time he was preparing to open his photographic studio on Washington Street in Columbia's "Little Harlem."

The early postwar interracial climate in Columbia was hostile enough to produce rumors of an impending Negro uprising so serious as to lead hundreds of white men "to arm and plan for assembling women and children in designated places," according to David Duncan Wallace in his book *South Carolina: A Short History, 1520-1948* (Chapel Hill: University of North Carolina Press, 1951). He reported that a committee of prominent citizens, again presumably white, "published a statement that they had investigated every rumor and found no 'organized attack' being plotted by Negroes." They "deprecated personal clashes and warned the Negroes against 'allowing violent and incendiary speakers, especially those from a distance.'"

Despite its obvious drawbacks, however, Columbia was also a city of at least some opportunity and security for all of its citizens, black and white. As one of the two chief urban centers for black South Carolinians, there was some safety in its numbers.

Columbia was an educational center for blacks, with Benedict College and Allen University, two private church-related schools which occupied adjacent campuses in the Waverley section of the city. Black historian Asa H. Gordon, in his *Sketches of Negro Life and History in South Carolina* (N.p., 1929), made the claim for Benedict that, although laboring constantly under the difficulty of securing enough money to support qualified black and white teachers and to develop its physical plant, it had "established an enviable reputation among the Negro colleges of America," with its emphasis "always placed upon thorough academic work."

Allen University's significance, wrote Gordon, lay primarily in the fact that "it was one of the earliest efforts on the part of the Negroes to help the Negro procure independent educational facilities under complete Negro control." In addition to Allen and Benedict, there was the Booker T. Washington School, which was founded in 1919 and which became for many years the only accredited Negro high school in South Carolina.

Moreover, Columbia was a relatively attractive city in which blacks, although segregated, could build comfortable homes. Many of the city's Negroes cared deeply about the quality of both their homes and their schools. Black journalist George S. Schuyler, after a visit to Columbia in early 1930, wrote in the *Pittsburgh Courier:*

> Here is a nice looking town where the Negroes have many creditable business concerns and scores of comfortable and attractive homes. Here also one finds what is all too rare in the South and North as well: a considerable circle of Negroes who read and can think, and are vitally interested in the play of ideas and the consideration of social, economic, educational and political questions. You can judge the intellectual stature of a community by what they show evidence of wanting to see and hear.

There were at least some black Columbians whose roots went back far enough into the city's history to provide them with pride in and affection for the place. Kelly Miller anticipated Schuyler's remarks when he wrote in his 1925 article in the *New York Messenger,* "The Negroes of my native state have had many ups and downs, but through it all they possess a courage and a determination to do worthwhile things." He went on to say, "They possess a coherence and attachment for the old state that time and distance cannot destroy. After all, we love to be known as a South Carolinian." A part of some blacks' basic identity as Columbians derived from their awareness that they had physically built the city.

Upon moving to Columbia from Fernandina, Richard S. Roberts paid $3,000 for a five-room house on a 200-foot-deep lot at 1717 Wayne Street. The fact that Roberts could purchase such a house is ample evidence that he and his family were members of a rising, relatively-affluent, middle-class black community. With its high ceilings and tall windows, the house possessed the innovative feature of a cold-water faucet, as well as electricity and a "flushing toilet." One clear light bulb at the end of a single cord hanging from the middle of the ceiling in each room supplied the light. Most blacks and numerous white families enjoyed no such amenities. Although the front yard of the house was small, the backyard was deep, extending to a fence that shut out a Pulaski Street mattress factory on the other side. In this lower part of the lot were fruit trees and a vegetable garden. In addition to an old barn, the backyard contained a 12 x 14 building detached from the main dwelling called the "little house." For about a year after moving to Columbia Roberts kept his equipment and supplies in the "little house" and used it for all of his photographic work except the actual taking of the pictures.

By 1922 Roberts had rented quarters for a photographic studio upstairs at 1119 Washington Street in the first block west of Main, an unpretentious second-floor area which he converted into a small suite suitable for his photographic purposes. The entire space measured approximately 12 x 20 feet and was divided into a waiting room hung with pictures he had made, a dressing cubicle, a general posing and work area, and a darkroom. Roberts was a self-taught photographer, who constantly educated himself through the literature he received from supply houses. During the 1920s and 1930s Roberts read such periodicals as *Studio Light,* published in Rochester, New York, by the Eastman Kodak Company, and advertised as "A Magazine of Information for the Profession"; *Photographic Bulletin,* published in Atlanta by the Eastman Kodak Stores there; *Snap Shots,* "A Monthly Magazine for Photographers" put out by the New York stockhouse of George Murphy, Inc.; and *Developments,* edited and published in Rockford, Illinois, by the Master Photo Finishers of America.

Roberts developed procedures and equipment not only to suit the limited floor space and poor natural light of the Washington Street quarters but also to implement techniques he had learned and continued to learn through the years. Regarding his father's technical and mechanical ingenuity Gerald Roberts has written:

> Much of the equipment he needed he improvised, such as the use of draperies and reflecting screens to enhance the image of the subject and control the shadows. He designed and constructed a hooded easel-like frame for retouching negatives, placing it at one of the many windows overlooking the street when using it. In the slanted area of the easel, he had provided a rectangular opening with an adjustable bar below it so he could place different sized negatives over the opening. A reflector on the opposite side of the window side of the easel played daylight through the negative so he could more easily

Unidentified portrait in studio frame.

see how to remove blemishes and wrinkles from the face of the subject, or put sparkle in the eyes, fill in unwanted shadows, or merely accent smoothness of lighting. He always kept four or five finely pointed pencils and a square of fine sandpaper for sharpening them ready to do his left-handed re-touching.

Roberts also designed and built a large artificial lighting cabinet which became an indispensable part of his studio equipment. Gerald describes this device as seven feet tall and five feet wide, containing four large blue electric bulbs which shone through a thin white fabric to diffuse the light and eliminate harsh shadows. It was mounted on rollers so that it could be moved around the posing area. No one remembers exactly how many cameras Roberts used in the studio, where they came from, or who made them. He had to have had cameras which could accommodate both 5 x 7 and 8 x 10 plates. His children remember that he had more than two, and that he owned and used different ones at different times. Among these, they recall, was a DeVry .31. Most of the portraits he made in the studio were in 3 1/2 x 5-inch format which could be used as postcards. Two of these photos could be made on one plate by the simple procedure of inserting a sliding frame of his design into the 5 x 7 plateholder, thereby permitting exposure of only half the plate at a time. The postcard portraits, which were in vogue at the time, he printed on commercially available emulsified cards. In addition to postcard-size studio portraits, Roberts also made many 5 x 7 pictures—in a choice of head-and-shoulder, three-quarter, or full-figure poses. Most of his 8 x 10 photographs were made outside the studio.

There were outside street displays drawing attention to the studio: a framed rectangular curbside sign with "Roberts Studio" written in large letters and the message "PERFECT PICTURES"; and three display cases. Advertisements for the studio appeared in the *Palmetto Leader,* as well as in printed announcements, programs, and yearbooks. A 1926 advertisement featuring a picture of the photographer himself encouraged interested persons to have "Beautiful Photographs" made at the Roberts Studio and indicated that the studio could "Copy, Enlarge, and Frame Pictures of any kind." Sittings were given "regardless of weather conditions" and patrons could be assured of "courteous and efficient service." December ads reminded readers that a photograph "is the gift that only you can give and no other gift will please so well." Roberts also issued, probably in the early 1920s, a four-page leaflet in which he detailed his services and philosophy as a photographer. He asserted that "a true likeness" of oneself was "just as necessary as every other necessity in life." To have one's photograph taken was a duty that one owed relatives and friends: "No other gift causes so much real and lasting joy to them as the gift of your photograph." "If you are beautiful, we guarantee to make your photographs just like you want them." "If you are not beautiful we guarantee to make you beautiful and yet to retain a true and brilliant likeness of you," he promised. He assured "proud and anxious" mothers that pictures of their babies and children were not hard to get, and guaranteed to make "cheerful and snappy photos" of every youngster who was brought into the studio. "We naturally love children: They are our friends." Their pictures should be taken, he said, on every birthday, so that when they were grown they would be able to see how they looked when they were young. "Arrange a sitting *today!*"

As for those who desired photographs made of parents and grandparents who could not be persuaded to visit the studio, the leaflet continued, "Leave them at home. . . . Engage us to make that sitting at home. We will respond with pleasure." It was stated that "proposals" were welcome from churches, schools, colleges, universities, and other institutions in and out of the city. "We promptly answer calls to do any kind of photographic work outside the Studio." Roberts always found a way to fill photographic requests from families in the black communities pocketing Columbia's outskirts: Arthurtown, Little Camden, Kendalltown. On the back of the leaflet the prospective customer was reminded that "PERFECT SATISFACTION" was guaranteed to everyone who called at the studio for service. "We accept no final payment on work until customers are fully pleased." His children remember that frequently Roberts would take a picture in a pose the customer wanted and then in one he wanted. Usually the customer would choose the photographer's pose.

The only surviving source of price information for work done in the Roberts Studio is found in a bound 11 x 14 sample book illustrated with different-sized photographs. This thin volume probably dates from the mid-1930s, near the end of Roberts's life or about the time when Gerald briefly took over the business. The homemade rate-book advertises three postcard portraits for $1.00; six for $1.25; nine for $1.50; twelve for $1.75 with 25¢ for each extra head, and 50¢ for each extra sitting. Normally, one could get three small photos— "for identification, gift, and album"—for 50¢. But a special deal was offered whereby a customer could purchase two small photographs plus an enlargement of his choice, according to the following price list: with an 8 x 10, $2.50; with a 6 x 8, $2.00; with a 5 x 7, $1.50; with a 4 x 6, $1.35; with a 3 1/2 x 5, $1.25,

Roberts advertised his posing hours as extending from 8:30 in the morning to 7:00 or 7:30 in the evening. This meant that he had to have someone to open up the studio and transact its business during the morning hours until he could get there at noon and then to assist him after he arrived, especially as the volume of business grew. Over the years, the studio was tended in the morning by a series of young women. Most of them lived with the Roberts family as part of the normal practice of "doubling up" during the economic push of the 1920s and the Depression of the 1930s. One such assistant, Janie Paris, a girl from nearby Irmo, worked in the studio during ten of its fifteen years, serving as receptionist, clerk, assistant photographer, and dressing-room attendant. In later years Gerald Roberts helped out. When an assistant was not available, Mrs. Roberts tended the studio.

The assistants must also have made some of the studio portraits. But all of the pictures which left the studio went out under the Roberts name; which studio assistants took which pictures, and how many, will never be known. However, the collection shows little variation in basic picture-taking style and approach. Whatever photographic technique was mastered by the assistants would have been learned under the tutelage of Roberts.

The subject of most of Roberts's pictures is the human image. The collection is made up largely of studio portraits. They are of persons of all ages, and of the living and the dead: Roberts was often called upon to make a casket portrait when the family realized too late that no likeness of their loved one existed. And they are from every social stratum in the black community—from the laborer and the domestic to the self-made entrepreneur and the educated professional. Roberts made many pictures of families at home—of the whole circle or of just the children—posed formally or informally sitting on the front porch or in the yard arranged on a bit of carpeting.

There are also a few architectural shots in the collection—of old homes or newly-built houses and institutional structures, especially schools. Furthermore, as the only black commercial photographer in the city, Roberts came to be depended upon for most of the "activities" and "events" pictures made at school, church, club, or other group gatherings—at class day or commencement exercises, commemorative occasions, work demonstration programs; of athletic teams, professional organizations, Sunday schools or whole congregations. Some of these appeared in the *Palmetto Leader,* which largely relied upon Roberts for photographs during the first ten years of its existence. In a sense, the fortunes and reputations of Roberts and the *Palmetto Leader* rose together during the decade from 1925 to 1935. Perhaps this was no accident. *Palmetto Leader* editor N. J. Frederick was Roberts's office neighbor across the hall on Washington Street.

Other communities in the state, as well as rural South Carolina, are represented in the collection. In 1924 Roberts acquired his first automobile, a second-hand Dodge touring car. His children remember going with him on picture-taking jaunts into the countryside as well as to other towns and cities around the state—to Irmo and Hopkins and Eastover close to home, and to places farther away: Florence, Ruffin, Charleston, and Johnsonville. On occasion he drove to some distant, isolated area on a picture-taking commission. In a surviving studio memo are these penciled directions: "Take the Anderson & Clemson highway after 12 miles you come to a town (Sandy Spring). After two miles you'll come to a town on the right turn to the left right there. After two miles of rough road you'll reach a hard surfaced dirt road after a quarter mile you'll come to a church in front is my house."

Probably during the fall of 1924, Roberts went to Orangeburg to take the class photographs of the 1925 *Wilkinsonian,* the first yearbook published by South Carolina State College. In

1926, he traveled to Greenwood to make a series of campus, student, and faculty pictures at Brewer Institute. And there are dozens of photographs of unidentifiable persons whose portraits have been made outside against Roberts's creased posing screen or against the weatherbeaten boards of rural homesteads, country churches, or one-room schoolhouses.

The collection takes on special interest as a documentary about the rise of the black middle class in South Carolina's capital city. Photographic records of plantation and Sea Island blacks have existed for years. But no comparable collection exists in South Carolina, in either published or unpublished form, to reveal the other face of the black community: that of the urban Negro of the 1920s and 1930s on the rise, going about the business of work and pleasure. Here are the carpenters, painters, plasterers, bricklayers, hotel bellmen, chefs, doormen, taxi drivers, chauffeurs; here are the merchants, domestics, dressmakers, barbers, beauticians, postal employees. Here, too, is the world of teachers and preachers and students, of doctors, dentists, pharmacists, midwives; of lawyers, insurance agents, businessmen, theater managers, newspapermen and morticians; and the housewives who were privileged and proud not to have to hire out to work for white people. And here are their children—always the children.

Roberts's photographs of course portray black Carolinians in their role as "burden bearers." But here also is W. E. B. Du Bois's "talented tenth" in South Carolina—the achievers, progressives, entrepreneurs who engaged in individual and communal programs of uplift and self-help, who were concerned not just with mere survival but "making it" and claiming their piece of the American pie. Roberts documented the lives of black South Carolinians in the creative and vital throes of their own Roaring Twenties and, later, in their determination to hang on through the Thirties. He cared about the truth in the images he made. There is the obvious, literal truth of social and economic history in his pictures: the evidence from dress and demeanor, from props and furnishings. The eye of the camera captures them all: the plain and the elegant, the poor and the prosperous, the stylish and the dull. Many of the subjects communicate flair and defiance, will and stubborn determination; a few, an earthy sensuality. On another level, some of the images reflect the weariness and sadness, the lethargy and hopelessness and resignation of deprived individuals.

But Roberts would have beauty as well as truth. While as a photographer he was himself an entrepreneur, principally he was an artist, a craftsman who cared about beauty of image, grace of form, balance and line, tone and contrast, the quality of light and the shades of darkness. His images are also studies in proportion and clarity. They combine both an attractive simplicity and a subtle complexity. The impact of his pictures derives in part from his own perfectionism, his determination to make his photograph as "right" as he could within the time limits of a posing session. Gerald remembers that details of posing "as trivial or minute as a particular fold in a garment, or the flex of a reclining finger" might consume many minutes of studio time. In the field, as well, Roberts paid the same kind of meticulous attention to detail. He would not take a group picture until every face could be clearly seen. With large groups, Gerald observes, his father evolved a system of having the subjects stand in an arc facing the camera, so that each figure or face would be in sharp focus. Roberts's perfectionism also showed up in the processing of the work. Gerald felt that at times his father wasted materials. When he suggested this to his father, Roberts replied that the artistry of the work came before conservation of supplies. The two continued to have debates about this, but the elder Roberts would not change.

The camera and the glass plate, then, became the means by which Roberts gave expression to the creative impulse within him. He was a visual artist at whose hand and eye the photographic form reached a peak of appealing art. While he may never have heard or used the term "Harlem Renaissance," or been aware of what it represented, his own creative life in Columbia paralleled what was happening in New York in the mid-1920s.

The value of the Roberts collection, and of the rediscovery of the work of this regional photographer, lies not only in its historical documentation of the rise of the black middle class in the urban but provincial center of a poor Southern state. And its value lies not only in its intrinsic aesthetic appeal as a photographic collection of undeniable technical finesse and formal beauty. Its power lies chiefly in its revelation—its true representation—of a lost world, of a people whose identity was lost not only upon the white world but also upon itself. Roberts's work, to be sure, opens up the world of the black Carolinian to the eyes of a white community which so often used it but never fully saw or knew it; but it also reveals the black community to itself.

In *One Time, One Place* Eudora Welty meditates upon the function of photography and ponders her own experience as a photographer during the 1930s. She speaks of her passion to "part a curtain, that invisible shadow that falls between people, the veil of indifference to each other's presence, each other's wonder, each other's human plight." That was Roberts's passion, too: not only to create a true likeness of each subject but also to communicate through his art a feeling of shared worth, a sense of value recognized and affirmed. The rediscovery of his photographs allows Richard S. Roberts to extend his concern. Here are his images, in all of the seriousness and richness of their presence, in all of the wonder and fullness of their humanity. Here, indeed, are his true likenesses and his own parted curtains.

*Acknowledgments:* This book could not have come into being without the support and encouragement of Richard S. Roberts's surviving children: Wilhelmina, Beverly, Gerald, Cornelius—and Cornelius's wife, Carrie. For their assistance every step of the way we express our gratitude.

A special word of thanks and recognition goes to the following Columbians who met repeatedly in an effort to identify subjects of the pictures, or who made themselves available, or went out of their way countless times to answer questions and to solve research problems related to the collection: Mr. Edwin Russell, Mrs. Dorothy Nance Russell, Mrs. Juliette Gilliam, Miss Priscilla Veale, Mrs. Modjeska Simkins, Mrs. Minnie W. Johnson, Miss Janie R. Creed, Miss Mary L. Little, Mrs. Catherine Hoover Fitzpatrick, Mr. Isaac C. Brown, Mrs. Rosella Benton, Mrs. Annie M. Smith, Mr. A. P. Williams, Mrs. Nancy Artemus Gough, Mrs. Montez Logan Bethea, Mrs. Billie Chappelle Stephenson, Mrs. Thomasina R. King, Dr. Sylvia P. Swinton, Mr. A. T. Butler, and the Reverend J. W. Witherspoon.

We also wish to convey our appreciation to other persons who assisted in the photo-identification project. In Columbia: Mrs. Fannie Phelps Adams, Mr. J. C. Artemus, Jr., Mr. and Mrs. James W. Artemus, Mrs. Elizabeth Ashford, Mr. C. Bruce Bailey, Mrs. Theodosia Ballen, Mrs. Ethel Johnson Berry, Mrs. Ethel M. Bolden, Mrs. Clarice C. Brandon, Mr. Louis C. Bryan, Mrs. Hortense Cooper Burley, Mrs. Jamestina Thompson Caldwell, Mr. Bill Canady, Mrs. Sarah Draft Clark, Mrs. Jennie C. Collins, Miss Harriett Mae Cornwell, Miss Vivian Counts, Mrs. Bernice Paul Crumby, Mrs. Frazelia Corley Crumlin, Mrs. Faleese Davis, Mrs. Anna Mae Dickson, Mr. Samuel Diggs, Dr. Percival L. Everett, Mrs. Anna Belle Johnson Eubanks, Mrs. Jessie Kennedy Fogle, Mr. William J. Gilliam, Mrs. Maxie Gordon, Mrs. Rita C. Gordon, Mrs. Sadie Adams Graham, Mrs. Rachel C. Griffin, Mr. and Mrs. Sanders Guignard, Mrs. Juanita Corley Hall, Mr. and Mrs. T. J. Hanberry, Mr. Kelly Miller Harvey, Jr., Mrs. Jessie Trottie Hill, Mrs. Vera L. Hill, Mr. Anthony Hurley, Mrs. Besse P. Jenkins, Mrs. Elise F. Jenkins, the Reverend Lincoln C. Jenkins, Judge Lincoln C. Jenkins, Jr., Mrs. C. A. Johnson, Mrs. Cecily Baxley Johnson, Miss Mary M. Jones, Mrs. T. B. Jones, Mrs. Emma Ruth Ray Kyer, Mrs. Virginia Vance Lemon, Mrs. Bertha Bouknight Lewis, Mrs. Mary G. Lilliewood, Mrs. Harriet T. Liverman, Mrs. Jennie Young McAdams, Miss Catherine E. Mack, Miss Frances A. Mack, Mrs. Marion Lover Marshall, Mrs. Celia Phelps Martin, Mrs. Lillian Holley Martin, Mrs. Natalie F. Martin, Mr. Thomas S. Martin, Mrs. Vivian N. Monteith, Mrs. Barbara Moore, the Reverend Rufus L. Mosby, the Reverend and Mrs. J. P. Neal, Mrs. Annie Greene Nelson, Mr. and Mrs. T. B. Nelson, Dr. Robbie Peguese, Mrs. Ruth Collins Perry, Mrs. Bertha Powell, Mrs. Marylyn Hoover Price, Miss Betty Reese, Mrs. Edna M. Reese, Mr. Christian C. Robinson, Dr. Harry B. Rutherford, Jr., Mrs. W. Gertrude Sanders, Mrs. Eloise Mosby Simons, Miss Theresa Singleton, Mr. and Mrs. Willie T. Smith, Dr. C. E. Stephenson, Dr. and Mrs. Edward Sweat, Mrs. Theodora Blocker Thomas, Mr. Daniel W. Thompson, Mrs. Myrtle S. Thompson, Mr. E. H. Trezevant, Mr. Sidney Trottie, Mrs. Fleda Jackson Turner, Miss Hattie Waiters, Mrs. Margaret S. Walker, Mrs. Delores Clark Washington, Mrs. Emily Clark

Washington, Mrs. Mary Shelton Washington, Mrs. Rosalyn Chappelle Weathers, Mr. Joseph F. White, Mrs. Lucy Williams, Mrs. Mary Louise Williams, the Reverend Bruce P. Williamson, Mrs. Ethel Wilson, and Mrs. Vashti Woodson.

Beyond Columbia, the following persons gave of their time and interest to the project: in Aiken, Mrs. George T. Cherry; in Allendale, Mrs. Thomasena H. Gardner; in Batesburg, Mrs. Martha Lavinia Scott Davis, in Beaufort, Mrs. Willidmina B. Barnwell, in Camden, Mr. Leroy Phillip Brisbane and friends, Dr. and Mrs. Theodore J. Whitaker; in Charleston, Mrs. Stephen B. Mackey, Mrs. Sadie Green Oglesby; in Denmark, Mrs. Jaynie Mae Shelton; in Eastover, Mrs. Janie Nickpeay Sims; in Georgetown, the Reverend H. B. Butler, the Reverend James E. Prioleau; in Greenville, Dr. Carroll V. Bing, Jr.; in Greenwood, Mrs. Robbie Mae Ebow, Mrs. Mary Lilla Dixon Heel, Mr. Benjamin Sanders; in Orangeburg, Mr. and Mrs. Thomas J. Crawford, Mrs. Gracia W. Dawson, Miss Edith Frederick, Mrs. Valeria Staley, Mrs. Carmen S. Thomasson, Mr. Clarence Tobin, Mr. Zack E. Townsend; in Spartanburg, the Reverend James B. Brown, Mrs. Genevieve Vincent Woodson; in Sumter, Mrs. Louise Bracey Bradley, Mr. and Mrs. George McCain, Mr. James T. McCain; in Trenton, Mrs. Ethel C. Blocker, Mrs. Patria Bettis Brayboy, the Reverend W. H. Hightower, Mr. and Mrs. C. W. Nicholson; and in Union, Mrs. Edna Jackson Gordon, Mr. Reginald Jackson, Mrs. Laura Whitney Jeter. Outside of South Carolina, these persons responded generously to requests for information and assistance: Dr. Naomi Garrett, Institute, West Virginia; Mrs. Bernice Randolph, Brooklyn, New York; Mr. John E. Jackson, Mount Vernon, New York; Mr. Hale B. Thompson, Jr., Jamaica, New York; and in Washington, D.C., Miss Sara Dunlap Jackson and Mrs. Crozer Carroll Taylor.

For their moral and practical support, we thank our respective University units: the South Caroliniana Library, Allen H. Stokes, Director; and the Department of Art, John O'Neil, Chairman. In addition, we wish to acknowledge the able assistance of students Valerie Bowen, Melissa Hines, and Elizabeth Roddey; and of Instructional Services photographer Phil Sawyer.

T. L. J.

P. C. D.

# A TRUE LIKENESS

Wilhelmina Pearl Williams Roberts (1881-1977), before 1920.  Roberts made this portrait of his wife at his Gem Studio in Fernandina.  Her daughter Wilhelmina has described Mrs. Roberts as a small, energetic, talented woman who "lived education," worked hard, and responded to the appeal of anyone in need.

Wilhelmina Telitha Minnie Roberts (b. 1915), ca. 1919. Roberts took many pictures of his children. This one, of his older daughter, was made in the Gem Studio. The seventh child of a seventh child, Wilhelmina was considered charmed by her mother. She graduated from St. Augustine's College in Raleigh in 1937 and from the Atlanta University School of Social Work in 1948. She was a caseworker with the Family Welfare Society in Columbia before moving to New York City, where she became established as a social worker, schoolteacher, and homemaker.

*Opposite:* Joseph Williams, probably 1920s. A part of the extended Roberts family in Columbia, "Uncle Joe" was Mrs. Roberts's brother. A former jockey, he drove a hack, drawn by a white horse.

The Roberts family with live-in students and studio assistants, ca. 1924. Mrs. Roberts insisted that her home be opened to take in young women from rural areas in South Carolina to enable them to attend high school in Columbia. Pictured in the back yard of the Robertses' home at 1717 Wayne Street beside their first car, a secondhand 1924 Dodge, are (seated, left to right) Martha Paris; Henry Hawkes, a cousin from Chicago; Cornelius Roberts; Miriam Roberts; Mrs. Richard S. Roberts; Wilhelmina Roberts; Richard S. Roberts; Mamie Verdier, a Florida friend; (standing) Beverly N. Roberts; Eva Lorick; Ethel Spence; Mattie Paris; Janie Paris; Leola Paris; Fannie Paris; and Gerald E. Roberts. The Parises were from Irmo, South Carolina, and Janie Paris assisted Roberts in the studio for many years.

Eliza James, 1920s. Master brickmason James and his wife Eliza were the Robertses' next-door neighbors at 1723 Wayne Street. She is photographed here in her front yard. Roberts's daughter Wilhelmina remembers that Mrs. James wore beautiful hats and long dresses that were either lavender or black and white.

Manigault-Gaten-Williams Funeral Home, ca. 1925-1927. Manigault's funeral home, located at 712-714 Main Street, was one of four black undertaking establishments operating in Columbia during the late 1920s. A Manigault Funeral Home continues in Columbia, under the direction of the founder's grandson, Anthony Hurley.

*Opposite:* Mr. and Mrs. William Manigault, 1920s. William Manigault (1883-1940) was a prominent Columbia mortician and owner of the Congaree Casket Company which reputedly employed more blacks than any other black-owned business in South Carolina. His wife, Annie Rivers (1892-1954), was called the "Belle of Ward One." The Manigaults lived a few houses down from the Roberts family on the same side of the street, at 1703 Wayne. The Manigaults may have been the first black family in Columbia to own a private swimming pool, which they built for their grandson, Anthony (Tony) Hurley, to play in as a boy.

Annie Mae Manigault (1907-1976), 1920s. After graduating from the Renouard School of Embalming in New York City, Miss Manigault came back to Columbia to work with her parents in the Manigault Funeral Home, launching a business career which lasted for fifty years. "We have a lady licensed Embalmer," local ads proclaimed. "When I started," she said many years later, "we worked out of the homes. In those days it was customary to work on a body in the house. I was young then and it didn't bother me much."

The Baylor Family, 1920s. With the Reverend Richard W. Baylor and his wife Delphine (seated) are Walter, Luther, and Bertie, three of their eight children. Baylor had been pastor of Zion Baptist Church from 1890 to 1913. Under his leadership church membership increased, a mortgage was paid off, and a parsonage was built. Columbia city directories of the 1920s show that during this period Baylor and his son Luther operated a grocery store in the same building in which they lived.

Mattie W. Holmes with nephew Holmes Lindsay in front of her residence, early 1920s. Mrs. Holmes, a widow, lived across from the Richland County jail. She owned rental property in Columbia and was driven by Lindsay in her 1919 Dodge sedan to collect the rents. Mrs. Holmes died in 1942 at the age of ninety-four.

Cornelius C. Roberts (b. 1913), ca. 1925. This is the only surviving picture of any of Roberts's studio cameras. His youngest son, Cornelius, has a plateholder in his hand. After graduating from the Hampton Institute Trade School in 1936, with a specialty in electrical science, Cornelius returned to Columbia and taught industrial arts, radio and electricity, and general shop variously in the city's junior high and high schools—until his retirement in 1975. Cornelius and his wife, Carrie, have maintained the family home at 1717 Wayne Street, where they cared for his mother until her death. Like his father, Cornelius has served St. Luke's Episcopal Church as a lay reader and has pursued an active interest in photography.

*Opposite:* Vernell Simons, 1920s. Vernell Simons worked as one of Roberts's studio assistants and lived with the photographer's family.

Blimp from a studio window, probably 1930s. This photograph provides the view of the south side of Washington Street which Roberts saw from his upstairs studio. The Ebaugh Seafood Market and the Baltimore Cafe can be seen at the lower left.

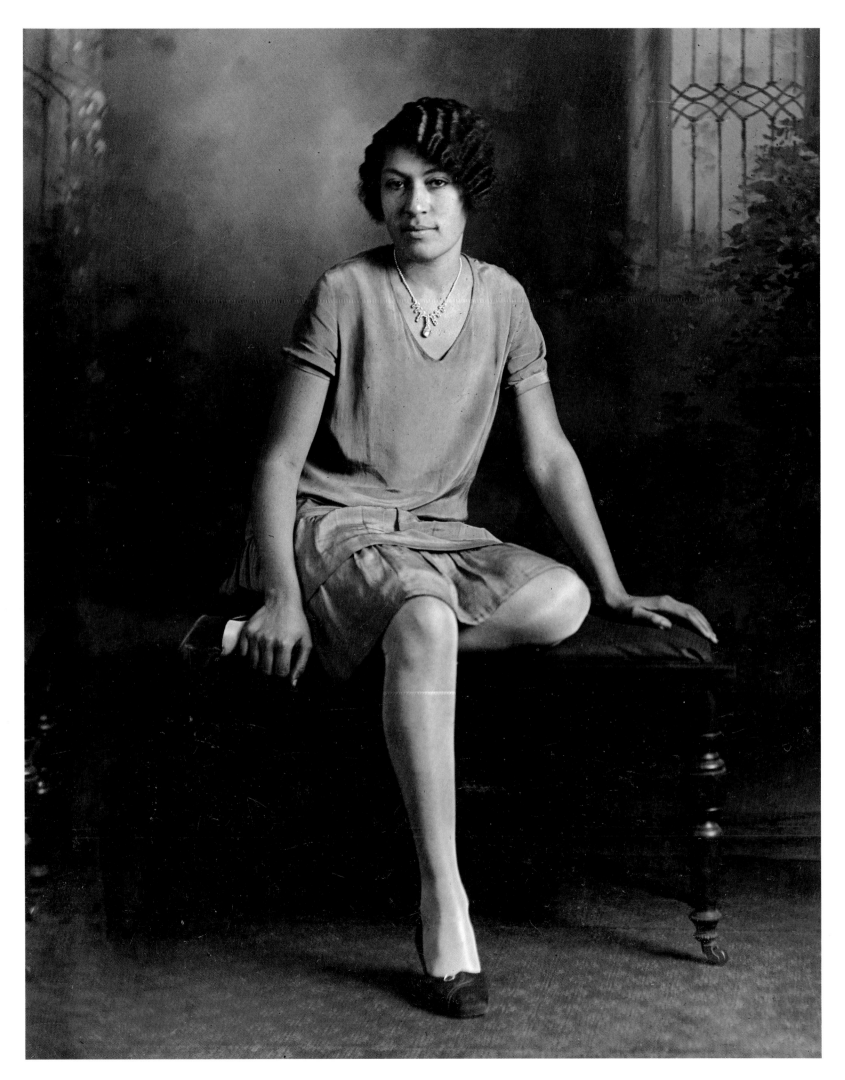

Unidentified portrait, 1920s. This photograph shows some of the photographer's essential studio furnishings and equipment, much of which he himself designed and constructed. The posing chair could be taken apart, enabling Roberts to use it with or without its decorative finials, back, or arms.

Unidentified portrait, 1920s. This photograph provides one of the clearest images of Roberts's studio backdrop, a large, romantic montage featuring tasseled drapery and a flowery pedestal by a drift of clouds on one side, a stylized cathedral window above a leafy motif on the other. This backdrop remained in use throughout the studio's fifteen-year existence. To the right is the photographer's homemade reflecting screen, which would have been cropped out of the client's finished print.

*Opposite:* Unidentified portrait, 1920s. Roberts often used the brocade-covered chair shown here in studio portraits.

Unidentified portrait, 1920s. The studio furniture included a bench which lent itself to the display of this subject's dress.

Unidentified portrait, 1920s.

Unidentified portrait, 1920s.

Unidentified portrait, 1920s. This young woman is wearing a fur piece, a studio prop that shows up in many of the women's portraits.

John E. Jackson, 1928. The year this picture was made, Jackson, the nineteen-year-old son of a Southern Railroad employee, graduated from the High School Department of Allen University. Seven years after the photo was made, Jackson left Columbia for New York. His suit was tailored by the local black firm of Owen and Paul.

*Opposite:* Unidentified portrait, 1920s.

Unidentified portrait, probably 1920s.

Unidentified portrait, 1920s.

Cromer Ware, probably early 1930s. From 1928 to 1937 Ware was a shoe shiner and porter in local barbershops, chiefly the Arcade Barber Shop at 1332 Main Street. From 1938 until his death (ca. 1953) he was a taxi driver, first with the Domino Taxi Club and then with the Blue Ribbon Taxi Club.

*Opposite:* Unidentified portrait, 1920s.

Unidentified portrait, 1920s.

Unidentified portrait, probably 1920s. The subject is holding a copy of the *State*, Columbia's morning newspaper.

Laura Goode (d. 1985), 1920s. Miss Goode was the daughter of James H. Goode, general manager of the Mutual Relief and Benefit Association in Columbia. Laura Goode wrote short stories which appeared in the *Palmetto Leader*, Columbia's black newspaper.

Alonzo P. Hardy, 1920s. Hardy, who was the son-in-law of Columbia mortician Thomas H. Pinckney, posed with a box camera, which was probably his own.

Unidentified portrait, 1920s.

Marion Evans, ca. 1930. Barber Marion Evans left Columbia for New York City. In the 8 March 1930 issue of Columbia's *Palmetto Leader* a notice appeared, along with this picture, advertising Evans's Sanitary Barber Shop at 79 West 131st Street, near the corner of Lenox Avenue. "When you are in New York City," the notice read, "visit the inventor of Evan's Hair Dressing."

Eliza Lovenia Neal Manigault (1896-1950), 1920s. Eliza Neal was among the oldest of sixteen children of the Reverend Jesse William and Minnie Holley Neal of Hopkins, South Carolina. In addition to preaching, her father worked his seventy-five-acre Lower Richland farm and taught for years in a one-room country school. Eliza graduated from Benedict College in 1918, married Winnsboro merchant and mortician Claude Manigault, and taught in the public schools of Fairfield and Chester Counties for thirty-two years.

Unidentified portrait, 1920s.

Unidentified portrait, 1920s.

George A. Elmore, probably late 1920s. At the time this picture was made, Elmore was probably a driver with the Blue Ribbon Taxi Club in Columbia. His would become one of the best-known names in the annals of post-World War II Southern legal and political history. He attempted to vote in South Carolina's all-white Democratic primary in August 1946. Denied the ballot, he agreed to become the "guinea pig" in a suit filed by the NAACP on 21 February 1947, in Federal District Court for the Eastern District of South Carolina against the manager of Columbia's Ward Nine and the Richland County Democratic Executive Committee, with John I. Rice named as defendant. Elmore's case was argued by Thurgood Marshall before Judge J. Waties Waring, who on 12 July ruled that the Democratic Party of South Carolina could no longer exclude qualified Negroes from participating in primary elections. Waring's decision destroyed the all-white primary in the state. Elmore, who from 1945 to 1948 was manager of the Waverley Five and Dime Store, reportedly became the victim of economic reprisals and neglect and by 1957 had disappeared from the scene. In 1981 a group of Columbia blacks erected a monument located just inside the upper entrance to the historic old Randolph Cemetery. The inscription reads:

Sacred to the
Memory of
GEORGE ELMORE
Who through Unmatched
Courage, Perseverance and
Personal Sacrifice Brought
The Legal Action by Which
Black People May Participate
in South Carolina Democratic
Party Primary Elections—
"Elmore vs. Rice," 1947.

Clyde Stevenson Yarborough (1903-1976), 1920s. One of five children of bricklayer Nicholas Stevenson and his wife Marion, Clyde Stevenson married North Carolina tailor Shannon Yarborough in 1918 and eventually moved with him to New York. Roberts made portraits of her on several occasions. "When they spoke of pretty girls," one of Miss Stevenson's contemporaries has remarked, "the Stevensons were always mentioned."

*Opposite:* Unidentified portrait, 1920s.

Unidentified portrait, probably 1920s. Beverly Roberts regards this photo as one of the "classiest" portraits his father made.

Unidentified portrait, probably 1920s.

Mr. and Mrs. George ("Big Five") Boyd, 1920s. Boyd (1895-1955) was a taxi and truck driver in Columbia. The woman with him here is believed to have been his first wife. No one remembers why he was given the nickname "Big Five."

*Opposite:* Unidentified portrait.

Unidentified portrait, 1920s.

Unidentified portrait, 1920s.

Unidentified portrait, 1920s.

*Opposite:* Unidentified portrait, probably 1920s.

Annie E. Plunkett, 1928. Mrs. Plunkett, portrayed here holding her three-month-old son John Wesley Plunkett, Jr., became better known as Annie Greene Nelson, one of the first black women novelists from South Carolina (*After the Storm*, 1942; *The Dawn Appears*, 1944; *Don't Walk on My Dreams*, 1961). She was educated at Voorhees Institute, Benedict College, and South Carolina State A&M College. She taught for eight years in South Carolina public schools, and for three years served as librarian at Waverley School in Columbia.

Unidentified portrait, probably 1920s.

"Po' Mary" with unidentified boy, 1920s. "Po' Mary" allegedly ran a series of "boardinghouses" in Columbia. She reputedly received her nickname because she charged twenty-five cents an hour for the use of a room.

The Carr Sisters, 1920s. Left to right, youngest to oldest: Clarice Ida, Rachel Pickens, Ethel Cyrine. These young women were daughters of Camden native "Captain" Alexander Carr, headwaiter at the Jefferson Hotel, and Mrs. Chaney Williams Carr, a Columbia midwife who had trained under the city's legendary white woman doctor, Jane Bruce Guignard. All three girls attended Benedict from elementary through high school. Mrs. Rachel Carr Griffin graduated from Benedict College in 1932 and taught for forty-two years in the public school system. Mrs. Clarice Brandon graduated from Benedict College in 1936, taught in Columbia and Kershaw County, and then went to New York, completed nurse's training, and worked as a nurse on Long Island. Mrs. Ethel Graham worked as assistant dietician at Benedict and then became owner and operator of a luncheonette.

*Opposite:* Unidentified portrait, 1920s.

*Opposite:* Unidentified portrait, probably 1920s.

Unidentified portrait, 1920s.

Unidentified portrait, 1920s.

*Opposite:* Unidentified portrait, 1920s.

Robert Harper Kennedy (d. 1972) and his nephew, Hale B. Thompson, Jr. (b. 1922), ca. 1927. Kennedy was a chef at Columbia's Jefferson Hotel before moving to Binghamton, New York, where he became chef-cook in a hospital. The boy was the son of Margaret Kennedy Thompson, whose husband was a mathematics professor, vice president, and dean of the college at Allen University. Educated at Johnston C. Smith and New York University, Thompson went on to become an educator and human resources administrator with the city of New York.

Jessie Kennedy (b. 1906), 1920s. Miss Kennedy, educated at Allen University, was an elementary school teacher in Columbia and Conway, South Carolina.

*Opposite:* Martha P. Grier (d. 1935) and her daughters, 1920s. Seated next to her mother is Lillie; standing, left to right, are Rose, Mamie, and Malinda. Mrs. Malinda Bolden, a schoolteacher, became the grandmother of astronaut Charles Bolden.

Thomas S. Martin (b. 1911), ca. 1925. Thomas Martin taught for thirty years at Booker T. Washington High School (1938-1968), where he coached the football, basketball, and tennis teams. His support of recreational education led to the introduction of physical education into Columbia's elementary schools and to construction of a public swimming pool for the city's black children. Beginning in 1970 he was activity director for the National Youth Sports Program held at the University of South Carolina, and in 1980 a city recreation park was named for him.

Unidentified portrait, 1920s.

Unidentified portrait, 1920s.

*Opposite:* Unidentified portrait, 1920s.

Unidentified portrait, 1920s.

Rebecca Hull Walton (d. 1931), 1920s. Member of an old Columbia family (the sister of civil rights activist Modjeska Simkins's mother, Rachel), Rebecca Hull married Charles L. Walton, one of the first black physicians in South Carolina. A schoolteacher and a well-known civic and social leader in the city, she helped raise money for the black sanatorium and was at various times director of the women's division of the black portion of the Community Chest drive and a member of the Governor's Committee for Relieving Unemployment. Mrs. Walton was also active in the Order of the Eastern Star, serving ultimately as Grand Royal Matron.

Unidentified portrait, 1920s.

Unidentified portrait, 1920s.

*Opposite:* Unidentified portrait, 1920s.

*Opposite:* Mrs. A. P. Williams (1884-1945) with her sons, A. P., Jr., and Fred, ca. 1927. This portrait was meticulously posed. Groceryman A. P. Williams, Sr., had died in April 1926, and Mrs. Williams took the best surviving picture she had of her husband to Roberts to see if he could patch it into a studio picture which the photographer would make of her and her sons, thereby creating a posthumous family portrait. Thus she stands to one side in what appears to be an ill balanced photograph. The final result survives in the Roberts collection. A. P., Jr., became a mortician; Fred, a businessman.

Unidentified portrait (copywork), 1920s.

Janie Paris, late 1920s. A farm girl from Irmo, South Carolina, Janie Paris worked in the Roberts Studio for about ten years as the photographer's assistant. She was paid five dollars a week and was given room and board at the Robertses'.

Richard S. Roberts, self-portrait, 1920s.

*Opposite:* Unidentified portrait, 1920s. Roberts advertised his willingness and ability to take his services to the client, and frequently went out into the community to photograph individuals or groups. He took along a portable backdrop which allowed the option of a carefully cropped, formal portrait.

Washington Street during a snow storm, ca. 1923-1926. This photograph, taken from a window of Roberts's studio, provides a westerly view of the south side of the street. Owen and Paul Tailors, whose sign appears in the foreground, occupied the ground floor in the building adjacent to the Roberts Studio.

The William H. Corley Family, 1920s. Postal worker Willie Corley and his wife Daisy are posed in front of their home with their children Bernard, Marjorie, Rudine, Meredith, Richard, and Eugene (held by his mother).

Unidentified portrait, 1920s.

*Opposite:* Unidentified portrait, 1920s.

Residence of Mr. and Mrs. Dennis H. Jackson II, 900 Harden Street, 1920s. An enterprising native of Lower Richland County, Jackson (1880-1948) came to Columbia about 1912. By 1914 he had established a grocery store behind his home, a one-story house on a half block in what is now the Five Points section of the city. As the business grew, so did the house (which still stands). Jackson became one of the most prosperous black merchants in Columbia, catering his business to a biracial clientele. For years, the Jackson home had the only telephone in the area, and neighbors used it in emergencies. Mr. and Mrs. Jackson had four children, grew prize-winning chrysanthemums in the front yard, and raised turkeys in the back. Jackson was one of the first blacks in the city to own a car—a Packard, which he hired out to local morticians at a rate of five dollars per funeral.

Man with a movie camera, 1920s.

*Opposite:* Unidentified child, 1920s.

Eugene R. Lewis and his sons, Melton and Eugene, Jr., ca. 1930. Lewis was a messenger with the U.S. Internal Revenue Department in Columbia.

Residence at the corner of Harden and Washington Streets, 1920s. Although somewhat altered in appearance, this house still stands.

Unidentified family, late 1920s. The car is a 1926 Buick.

J. C. Artemus, Sr. (1885-1964), probably 1920s. The son of freed slaves who became sharecroppers, Artemus left his native Edgefield County in 1907 and came to Columbia, where he found work with local merchants, attended evening classes at Benedict College, learned carpentry, and became an agent with the North Carolina Mutual Insurance Company. During the Depression, he took up carpentry full time, and in 1939 was instrumental in organizing a black carpenters' union in Columbia. He became involved in politics and served as treasurer of the South Carolina Progressive Democratic Party, an alternative organization established in the 1940s to give a political voice to blacks and other South Carolinians who were disenchanted with the white-controlled election process in the state. Eventually he became a leader in regular party politics, serving as vice president, election officer, and poll manager of Ward Nine. Artemus was also active in church and fraternal affairs

The Artemus children, 1923. This picture of the Artemus children—Louise (age twelve), James (age five), Mary (age ten) holding one-year-old J. C., Jr., Nancy (age three), and Julia (age eight)—was taken in front of their home.

*Opposite:* Unidentified portrait, 1920s.

Children in costume, 1920s. Roberts was called to the home of a Columbia dressmaker for this picture. Her sign is in the window at left.

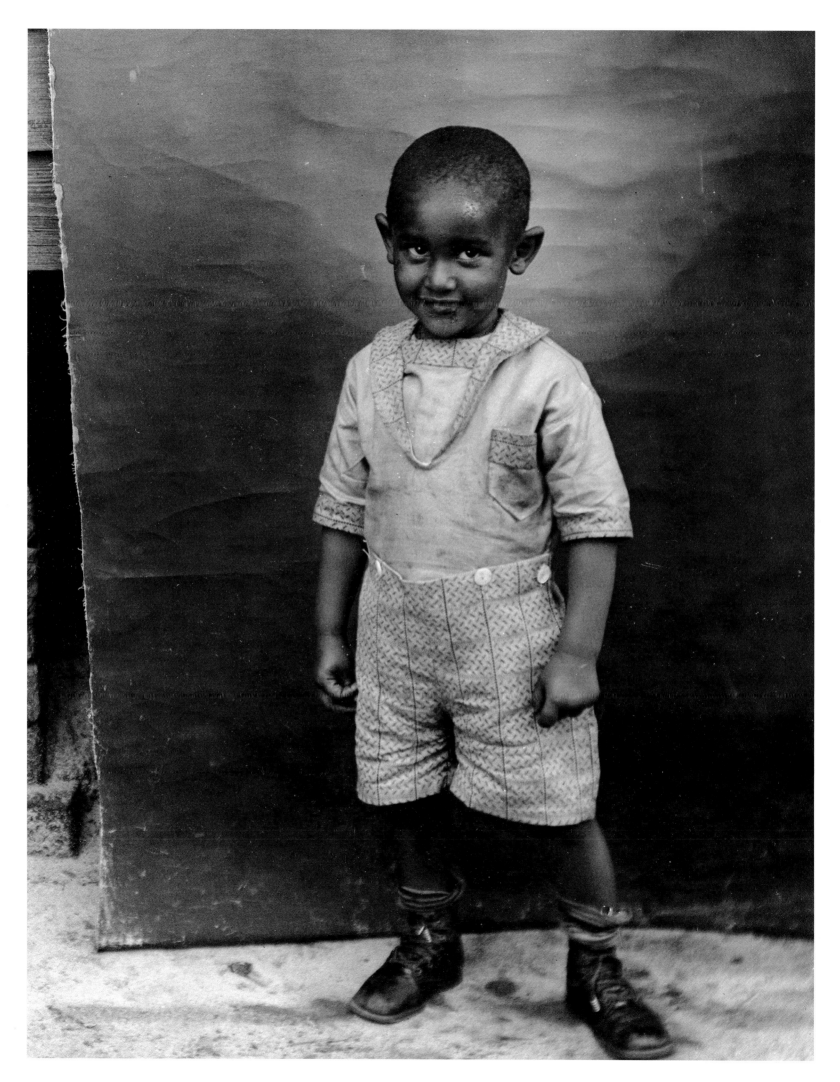

Mrs. Inglesby (?), probably 1920s. Roberts took a series of photographs of this woman wearing formal attire and surrounded by her antique furnishings.

Residence and subjects unidentified, 1920s.

Daniel and Jamescina Thompson in their yard, ca. 1923. The children of Columbia tailor James W. Thompson (1885-1966) and his wife Ruby (1888-1953).

Unidentified portrait, 1920s.

Unidentified portrait, 1920s.

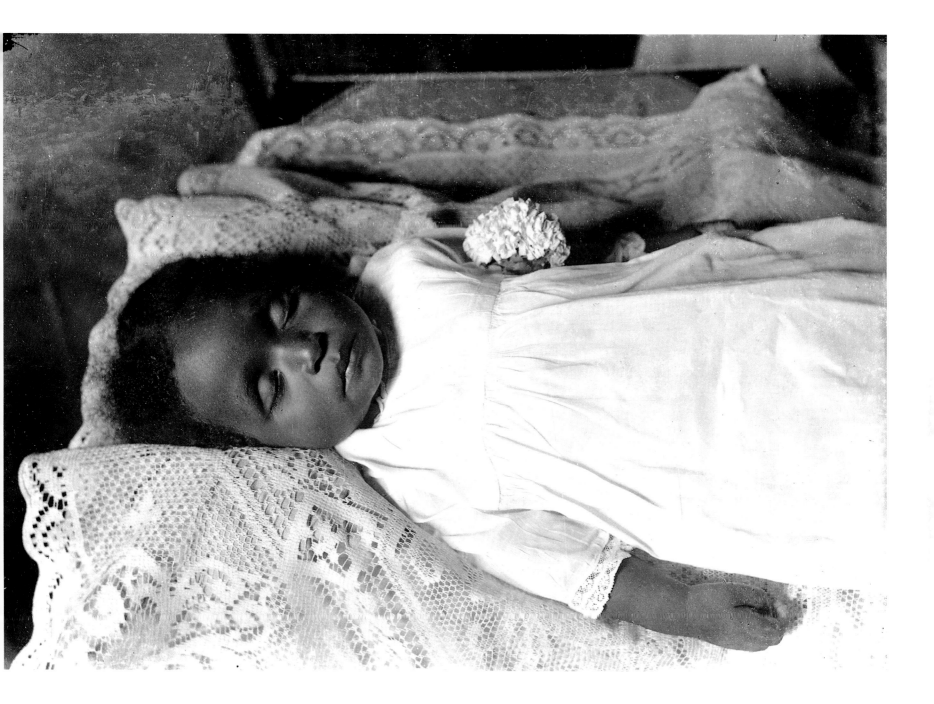

Portrait of an unidentified deceased child, probably 1920s.

*Opposite:* Unidentified portrait, 1920s.

Workers on a construction project, probably early 1930s.

Unidentified portrait, probably 1920s. This woman had her photo made two ways: in her maid's apron, and with jewelry.

*Opposite:* Unidentified portrait, 1920s.

Unidentified portrait, 1920s.

Unidentified portrait, 1920s.

Unidentified man outside Simons Body Works, ca. 1929-1930. With a decade of experience as a wheelwright and blacksmith, Robert L. Simons established Simons Body Works in 1929.

Charles McKeever, 1926. This picture appeared on the front page of the *Palmetto Leader* on 17 April 1926, when it was announced that McKeever, of Nashville, had been named the new manager of the Royal Theatre in Columbia. "Mr. McKeever," the accompanying notice read, "is not a novice in the moving picture business. He will continue to give the public high-class motion pictures and other interesting programs."

*Opposite:* Charles S. McIntosh, 1920s. McIntosh was a carpenter in Columbia for at least twenty-one years (1921-1942). He helped organize a black carpenters' union in in the city (Local No. 2260) in the late 1930s, and served as its treasurer. He also was one of the first black taxi drivers in Columbia. A 1939 city directory lists him as manager of the Diamond Taxi Club.

A Julep Line driver with his truck, ca. 1924 to 1926. The driver of this soft-drink truck was probably making a routine delivery at Williams' Drug Store. To the right is the sanctuary of First Nazareth Baptist Church.

Unidentified chauffeur, 1920s. Local black chauffeurs had formed their own organization by the early 1930s. The Palmetto Chauffeurs Club met monthly, collected dues, and urged every commercial automobile and truck driver in Columbia to join the group.

Angeline E. Evans, 1931. This portrait was published in Columbia's *Palmetto Leader* on 16 May 1931 at the top of an advertisement announcing Miss Evans's services in her home as a dressmaker and seamstress. By December of that year the picture was appearing in an advertisement for the Angie Evans Dress Making and Art Shoppee and listing some of her specialty items for sale: boudoir dolls, vanity sets, ladies' dance handkerchiefs, door stops, ash trays, boudoir pillows, men's silk handkerchiefs, sport scarfs for women and misses, window shades including mats to match. She also carried "a plain line of ready to wear."

William Veale (1905-1960), probably 1920s. Willie Veale lived with his grandmother, Mrs. Ophelia White, a block away from the Robertses. A painter and plasterer, he grew to be six feet, eight inches tall and was able to do much of his work without a ladder. Roberts's daughter Wilhelmina remembers that Willie Veale painted the walls of their home at 1717 Wayne Street. "He did a good job, taking extra care to stipple the living room in blue, pink, green and yellow, using sponges to make the walls look like flowered wallpaper."

Hazel Gibson Bookman (d. 1975), probably late 1920s. After graduation from Benedict College, Mrs. Bookman became secretary-cashier for the National Benefits Life Insurance Company and later bookkeeper for Waverley Hospital. Mrs. Bookman entertained Marian Anderson in her Gadsden Street home following the singer's appearance at Allen University in the late 1920s.

Manning H. Baxley (1899-1980), 1920s. With only about a fourth-grade education, Baxley left his native Barn-well County as a young man, went to Pittsburgh to work in the steel mills, and soon returned South to seek his fortune in Columbia, arriving with less than a dollar in his pocket. After working at odd jobs and serving as an orderly at the State Hospital, he eventually owned and operated, at different times, a restaurant-filling station, two dairies, a grocery store (which still exists), and later a nursing home and a motel.

Eddie Hoover Mosby (d. 1945), ca. 1930. Son of a railroad man who had been born in Ireland, Mosby owned and operated a barbershop. Seven of the eight Mosby brothers were barbers.

Benjamin Allen Blocker (ca. 1884-1960), 1920s. A native of Fairfield county, Blocker graduated from Allen University, taught school, and eventually opened a dry cleaning establishment. He was one of the first blacks in the area to own his dry cleaning equipment.

*Opposite:* Martha Lavinia Scott (b. 1909), 1927. The Scotts and Robertses knew each other through their membership in St. Luke's Episcopal Church. Miss Scott's father was a masonry contractor; her mother, part Croatan Indian, was a teacher and seamstress, from whom Miss Scott learned how to sew expertly. Educated in Greensboro, North Carolina, and at Benedict College, she married tailor William Lester Davis of Batesburg in 1931, moved there with him, taught elementary school, and assisted in the tailoring business. She and her mother made the dress Miss Scott is wearing.

Matilda Griffin, 1920s. This well-respected Columbia matriarch was known affectionately as "Mother Griffin." A Gold Star Mother who lost two sons in World War I, she is best remembered for the building she erected in their memory and for her determination to organize a veterans' post in Columbia. The post was officially established in April 1930, with an initial membership of seventeen veterans. For many years she supervised an Armistice Day program, held at Benedict College, in commemoration of the part played by black Americans in World War I.

Eliza Griffin Perrin Ratliff, 1920s. Matilda Griffin's daughter, Eliza, was married twice—first to the Reverend Robert M. Perrin of Allen University and then to businessman G. Lee Ratliff. She was a teacher in Benedict College's elementary school and gave private piano lessons.

The Reverend M. H. Holloway, ca. 1926. In 1926 the Reverend Holloway established a business school upstairs in the Griffin Memorial Building, offering the "opportunity to take a Business Course in Typewriting, Shorthand, Book-keeping and Millinering." The course cost fifty or sixty dollars, depending on whether one paid twenty-five dollars upon entering and twenty-five dollars at the end of the first month or five dollars per week. He also operated the Taylor Street Quick Lunch in the Griffin Building beneath the business school, and maintained an auto repair shop in the rear.

Griffin Memorial Building, ca. 1926. Matilda Griffin had this structure erected at a cost of $7000 in honor of her two sons, Sgt. Samuel H. Griffin and Clifton Griffin, who died in World War I. "Perhaps Mrs. Griffin is the first of both white and colored women, and men too, for that matter, for we have not heard of another, who has tho't of such a beautiful tribute to their sons," wrote the editor of the *Columbia Record-Indicator* in August 1926. Gov. Thomas G. McLeod delivered an address at dedication services for the building held in the Benedict College chapel on 11 November 1926. The house to the left was the home of Dr. Matilda A. Evans.

*Opposite:* Henry D. Pearson (1892-1954), 1920s. By the time he was fifteen, Henry Pearson had become the sole support of his mother, two sisters, and a brother. Starting out as a special delivery messenger boy in 1907, he later worked as a clerk with several Columbia grocery stores and as a tailor for I. S. Leevy before becoming a letter carrier with the post office in 1914. By 1930 the Champion and Pearson Funeral Home had been established and within four years it bore his name only. There is also evidence that Pearson tried his hand at commercial photography. A photograph survives in the hands of one of his daughters with the logo "Joyce and Pearson" printed on its folder. Pearson married Berverlina Nash Thompson, whose grandfather, William Beverly Nash, had been a black state senator in South Carolina. The Pearsons became the parents of six children, three boys and three girls. During the 1920s they lived in a large house on a block Pearson owned in the Wales Gardens section of Columbia. Pearson also acquired a fifty-six-acre country place five miles from the city, which he used as a summer home and where he grew flowers as a hobby.

A Columbia funeral, ca. 1926. The funeral here is probably being conducted by the firm of Manigault-Gaten-Williams; Mrs. Manigault appears to be the figure in the distance behind the coffin. S. P. Wheeler, an Allen University carpenter and steward of Bethel A.M.E. Church, is the gray-haired pallbearer facing the camera behind the casket to the right. The curtains in the simulated windows in the hearse are actually carved wood.

Unidentified funeral portrait, 1920s.

Unidentified portrait, 1920s.

Dr. Matilda A. Evans (1870s-1935), ca. 1930. As a student at Schofield Normal and Industrial School in Aiken, Matilda Evans became a protégée of the school's Quaker founder and leader, Miss Martha Schofield, who encouraged her to go on to Oberlin College and ultimately to the Woman's Medical College of Pennsylvania, where she received an M.D. degree in 1897, the only black in her class. That year she moved to Columbia and set up practice as a physician and surgeon. She treated both blacks and whites, established the first black hospital in Columbia, and founded the South Carolina Good Health Association to spread the word of the importance of good health practices and sanitation. In 1930 she opened a free clinic where poor black children could be treated and vaccinated. She introduced medical examinations into the public schools of Columbia. Although she never married, she adopted and reared eight children.

Nurses outside the home of Dr. Matilda Evans, 1920s. These four nurses probably trained under or assisted Dr. Matilda Evans, whose name appears on the sign next to the mailbox in the upper left-hand side of the picture. The nurses are, left to right: Gretchen Evans, Sarah Green, Elizabeth Harris, and Mattie Evans. In the window in the upper middle part of the photograph, observing the scene, is Dr. Evans's grandnephew Edward Evans.

*Opposite:* Dr. Matilda Evans's Pond at Lindenwood Park, ca. 1926. There were no public recreational facilities for blacks in Columbia in the 1920s. During the summer of 1926 Dr. Evans announced the opening of Lindenwood Park on property she owned. The Lindenwood complex featured a swimming pond, dance hall, and the Blue Bird T Room. "Come out Swim, Dance, Eat and Enjoy the Cool Breezes," read an ad in the *Palmetto Leader* on 17 July 1926.

Unidentified group at a meeting of the State Nurses' Association, probably early 1930s. During the period Roberts was taking pictures there were three black hospitals in Columbia with schools of nursing: Good Samaritan (1910-1939), Benedict (1914-1926), and Waverley (1924-1939). News coverage of the activities of the Graduate Nurses' State Association began at least as early as 1926, when an article in Columbia's *Palmetto Leader* on 7 August reported on the association's spring meeting held on the campus of Benedict College. The organization's motto was summed up in one word: "cooperation."

Residence of Dr. B. A. Everett, 1329 Pine Street, 1920s. Dr. Everett maintained his office in a separate building behind the house.

Dr. Benjamin A. Everett (1886-1965), 1920s. A native of Texas, Dr.
Everett finished Meharry Medical College, Nashville, in 1912 and came to
Columbia in 1913. He was one of six black doctors practicing in the city at
that time.

*Opposite:* Dr. Norman A. Jenkins (1882-1935), ca. 1929. Educated at Benedict College and Shaw University Medical School at Raleigh (1908), Jenkins practiced medicine and was a businessman in his native city of Anderson from 1908 until 1920, when he moved his medical practice to Columbia. He founded and superintended the Waverly Fraternal Hospital and Nurses Training School. He was active in Columbia's black professional, church, fraternal, and business affairs, and organized one of the first black recreational centers in the city.

Ethel C. Stephenson (1900-1956), 1920s. A native of Rock Hill, Ethel Crawford moved to Columbia at an early age with her mother, who was a seamstress. At twenty-one Miss Crawford married Dr. Charles E. Stephenson, many years her senior, and became a homemaker and the mother of two sons.

A graduating class, Good Samaritan Hospital Nurse Training School, probably late 1920s. The Good Samaritan Hospital, founded in 1910 by Dr. and Mrs. Swan Rhodes, was one of two black hospitals in Columbia in the late 1920's that had a school of nursing.

Janie R. Creed (b. 1907), ca. 1926.  A native of Leesville, Miss Creed graduated in 1926 from the Nurse Training School of Good Samaritan Hospital and became a public health nurse.

Booker T. Washington High School, Class of 1933. This photograph was taken in front of the main entrance to the school, looking north toward what is now part of the campus of the University of South Carolina.

*Opposite:* Mrs. Celia Dial Saxon (1857-1935), 1920s. When she died, Celia Dial Saxon was eulogized as "probably South Carolina's best known and most beloved woman of our race and one of our most outstanding educators." Born and reared in Columbia, she attended the University of South Carolina during Reconstruction and spent fifty-seven years serving in the city's public schools. Mrs. Saxon served as treasurer of the Palmetto State Teacher's Association and was active in the Federation of Negro Women. She was also one of the founders of the Fairwold Industrial School for delinquent Negro girls and the Wilkinson Orphanage of Negro Children. During her lifetime a school was named for her. After her death Saxon Homes, a city housing project, was also named in her honor.

Booker T. Washington High School football squad, Fall 1932. (Front) mascot Norman (last name unknown); (first row) Isaac C. Brown, Leroy "Tony" Shelton, George Phelps, George Kershaw, Jasper Byrd; (second row) J. D. Robinson (on brick wall), Alex "Peter" Walker, Marion Williams, *unidentified*, Arthur Cooper, Mimnaugh Amos, James Whitman, Joe White, Moses Hopkins (on brick wall); (third row) Roosevelt Franklin, Robert Watson, *unidentified*, William Lawson, Chris Robinson, Boston Brice; (top row) Coach Leslie Stallworth, Principal J. Andrew Simmons. Stallworth was teacher of physics. University of South Carolina's freshman "Biddie" team gave the Booker T. Washington squad its used equipment. The object in front of the mascot is a helmet; the football that was to have been used in this photograph had just been stolen.

Beverly Nash Roberts (b. 1911), ca. 1925. The fifth of the Roberts children was named for black
South Carolina state senator William Beverly Nash. An eighth grader at Booker T. Washington
High School when this photograph was made, Beverly is wearing the first suit he ever bought for
himself, purchased for thirty dollars on layaway with money he earned delivering newspapers. He
graduated from Benedict College in 1932 and left for New York to find work and pursue his
education. After receiving an M.A. degree in English education from New York University, he
taught for nine years at North Carolina A. & T. College in Greensboro and then in the New York
public schools, principally at Frederick Douglass Junior High School in Harlem, where he took over
Countee Cullen's creative writing class after the poet's death. He retired as an administrator for the
New York school system in 1978.

Modjeska Monteith, ca. 1923-1924. When this portrait was made, Miss Monteith was teaching six classes of algebra a day—four sections for beginners, two for second-year students—at Columbia's Booker T. Washington School. While she is also remembered for her later work in helping to stamp out tuberculosis in South Carolina and as a successful businesswoman, Modjeska Monteith Simkins became best known as a persistent fighter for social justice and civil rights and as one of the most determined and outspoken advocates of racial equity in the state.

William Augustine Perry (1883-1938), ca. 1928. With degrees from Yale (A.B., 1907) and Harvard (M.A. in Education), William Perry came to Columbia in 1928 to take charge of the Waverley School. Columbia's Perry Middle School bears his name.

*Opposite:* M. Crozer Carroll, 1920s.  Miss Carroll was the daughter of the Reverend Richard Carroll (1859-1929), a Baptist minister from Barnwell, South Carolina, who became known as one of the most persuasive black voices in the state.  She graduated from Benedict College in 1922 and studied at Oberlin College and Columbia University (M.A., 1931) before returning to Benedict to teach English and Latin.

Benedict College Baseball Team, 1931.  First row (standing, left to right): Walter Dean, Roy Finley, Bus Williams, Ernest Hughes, Allen Coles, Holmes Thompson; back row (left to right): William Hill, Archie Sloan, Samuel Diggs, Livingston McFarland.  In front, at left, next to the unidentified bat boy, is Coach Jack Williams.

Julia A. Starks (1873-1953), probably early 1930s. Along with her husband, the Reverend J. J. ("Buddy") Starks, who in 1930 became the first black president of Benedict College, "Ma" Starks (as the students called her) was one of the pioneers of higher education for blacks in South Carolina. The Starkses served together for forty-seven years, first at Seneca Institute in Seneca, South Carolina, then at Morris College in Sumter, finally at Benedict, where she functioned not only as hostess but also as dean of women. She was a graduate of Clark College, Atlanta University.

Zack Townsend and his family, ca. 1929-1930. Townsend (1891-1967) graduated from Benedict
College in 1921 and returned there to teach mathematics in the college and high school from 1923 to 1933. He
later served as principal of the black elementary school in Aiken, and then taught at Bettis Academy in Trenton,
South Carolina, and Morris College in Sumter. He was a leader in the Prince Hall Grand Lodge of Free and
Accepted Masons. With him here are his wife, Amanda (1892-1970), and three of his four children: Ruth
(1924-1973), Harold (1926-1981), and Naomi (b. 1928).

Gerald E. Roberts (b. 1909), 1931. After graduation from Benedict College in 1931, Gerald helped his father in the studio until 1935, by which time the Depression had practically wiped out Roberts's photographic business. He went to New York when he was denied a job with the Columbia post office (despite qualifying with a top rating) and picked up whatever odd jobs he could find—winding up as a waiter on a Pennsylvania Railroad dining car—before accepting an offer of federal employment in Washington, D.C. Starting as an elevator operator in the Veterans Administration Building, he moved on to the Department of the Interior in 1939, where he received a professional rating, and stayed there until 1978, serving variously as an assistant to the law librarian, acting law librarian, departmental acquisitions librarian, and finally as gift and exchanges librarian. Since 1978 he has been with the library of the Department of Labor.

Ruth Bynum, 1920s. After graduating from Benedict College, Miss Bynum taught in Columbia public schools.

Chappelle Administration Building, Allen University, ca. 1922. Founded in Cokesbury, South Carolina, in 1870, Payne Institute was moved to Columbia in 1880 and took the name Allen University in honor of Bishop Richard Allen (1760-1831), founder of the African Methodist Episcopal Church. Owned and controlled by blacks since its beginning, Allen University advertised itself in the 1920s as an accredited coeducational institution offering exceptional opportunities to Negro youth. In this architectural study, Roberts has photographed the Chappelle Building, probably in the final stages of its completion. Designed by John Anderson Langford (1874-1946), who has been called "the dean of black architects," the building was named for Bishop W. D. Chappelle, a former president of Allen.

*Opposite:* The Reverend Dr. George A. Singleton, 1920s. Born in Conway, South Carolina, in 1894, George Singleton received his high school and college education at Allen University, graduating from the latter with first honors in 1916. After World War I, he was ordained as a minister in the African Methodist Episcopal Church and became one of the most highly educated and well-respected leaders in that denomination. He received A.M. and S.T.B. degrees from Boston University, a D.B. from the University of Chicago, and studied at Harvard. Wilberforce University and Payne and Edward Waters colleges awarded him honorary degrees. This picture of Singleton was probably taken sometime between 1923 and 1925 while he was a professor of Social Science at Allen.

Allen University, Normal Department honor graduates, 1921. Allen's Normal Department consisted of teacher training courses which called for two years of study beyond four years of high school. Students who graduated from this department received an "L.I." diploma—the Licentiate of Instruction degree, which enabled them to teach. In 1921 fifty-five students graduated from Allen's Normal Department. Among this honor group are (seated, left to right) Alethia Aderson, *unidentified,* Charity Nance, *unidentified,* Marie Waymer; (standing) Angeline Grant, *unidentified,* Helen Smith, Birdie Pompey, Corrine Trezevant, and Ed Murray.

The Reverend F. Norman Fitzpatrick, D.D. (d. 1967), probably early 1930s. Born in Barbados, but reared in Puerto Rico, South America, and New York, Fitzpatrick, a cum laude graduate of Howard University, taught in Oklahoma and New York before coming to Allen University in 1930, where he spent the remaining thirty-seven years of his life. At Allen he taught a variety of subjects, notably in the College of Education and in the Dickerson Theological Seminary. Trained as an Episcopal priest, he eventually served as Dean of the College of Liberal Arts and Sciences at Allen. He married Catherine L. Hoover, daughter of a well-known Columbia merchant.

A baseball game at Allen University's Hurst Field, probably late 1920s.

Three professors, Allen University commencement, 1933. These three men—the Reverend Rip Isaiah Lemon (1892-1962), Robert L. Peguese (1892-1960), and Herbert W. Baumgardner (1897-1952)—were close friends as well as Allen colleagues. Lemon held a theological degree from Boston University, taught Hebrew and New Testament Greek in Allen's Dickerson Theological Seminary; Peguese was principal of Allen's High School Department and taught English; Baumgardner taught high school and college level German and English in the College of Liberal Arts and Sciences.

*Opposite:* Jennie Young (b. 1903), before 1927. This portrait of Miss Young was made while her father, the Reverend Calvin M. Young, Sr., was president of Harbison Agricultural and Industrial School, a Presbyterian-related institution located twelve miles west of Columbia at Irmo. She spent most of her life doing educational work in administration and teaching—most of it at Harbison, where she was serving as dean of students when the school closed in 1958.

The Reverend Dr. John G. Porter (1878-1948), probably late 1920s. From 1929 to 1941 Porter was president of Harbison, which was considered the hub of vocational education in Lexington County, near Columbia.

Bishop Reverdy Ransom and the State Presiding Elders of the African Methodist Episcopal Church, probably 1932. The figures in this photograph have been identified as follows: (first row, standing, left to right) J. M. McKenzie Harrison, T. J. Miles, Mrs. Reverdy Ransom; (seated) the Right Reverend Reverdy Ransom; (second row) *unidentified*, A. P. Spears, Sandy Simmons, I. W. Wilborn, M. A. Hollins; (seated) L. R. Nichols; (third row) L. H. Hemmingway, E. A. Adams, G. K. Lyles; (fifth row) J. E. Brogdon, D. H. Sims, E. Philip Ellis.

*Opposite:* The Reverend and Mrs. Henry M. Moore, ca. 1921 to 1925. Henry Moore was pastor of the Second Calvary Baptist Church from 1921 to 1925. He also taught at Benedict College during the 1923-1924 school term.

The Reverend Sarah H. Smith (1884-1937), 1920s. Sister Smith came to Columbia from Savannah early in the century and preached from corner to corner and house to house. In 1913 she organized the Bethlehem Baptist Church, which still exists. In a 1926 article in the *Palmetto Leader,* Bethlehem Baptist was identified as the third largest congregation in the city, and Sister Smith as "the greatest woman-preacher in the country," who had "organized and built the church from the ground herself in the face of severe opposition."

The Reverend Charles Jaggers (1831-1924), early 1920s. Jaggers was a self-proclaimed minister who, because of his constant and selfless attention to the needs of the helpless and destitute in the black community, was beloved in Columbia. Born a slave in Fairfield County, Jaggers was hired out for five years at the age of nine. At the age of fourteen, while working as a cart driver on the grading of the Charlotte railroad, he experienced a religious conversion and immediately began preaching. Although injured at work on the railroad, he carried on a life of religious and humanitarian service, which included preaching to prisoners and soliciting support for the Colored Orphanage in Columbia. He established and worked tirelessly on behalf of the Jaggers Old Folks Home, the city's only home for elderly blacks at the time. A short man who customarily wore a Boston Dipper and an old Prince Albert coat, Jaggers made his rounds carrying a Bible in his left hand and a walking stick in his right. A local sculptor, T. I. Weston, made a bronze statue of him which can be seen at the Columbia Museum. At the time of his funeral the county court was adjourned and, upon proclamation of the mayor, Columbia businesses closed their doors. The services at Bethel A.M.E. Church were attended by thousands, including elected officials, bank presidents, paupers, and ex-convicts.

The ushers of Union Baptist church, Columbia, 1933.

*Opposite:* The Reverend Lincoln C. Jenkins (b. 1888), ca. 1928. During the 1920s Jenkins served as pastor of the Unity Baptist Church and as principal of the black public school in the town of Kershaw, some sixty miles northeast of Columbia, living there during the school term but maintaining a permanent home in Columbia. He later pastored Columbia's Union Baptist Church for forty-eight years.

*Opposite:* Eva Prioleau Trezevant (1903-1984), ca. 1927. Mrs. Trezevant was a charter member of St. Martin de Porres Catholic Church, an education- and service-oriented congregation established in Columbia in 1935. A graduate of Allen University, she served in the public school system for forty years, retiring in 1968. She was an active clubwoman and civic leader.

Board of Deacons, Second Calvary Baptist Church, ca. 1925. This is one of several photographic composites Roberts made of Second Calvary officers and organizations. The deacons here are: (top row) Alfred Love and Robert W. Jackson, (middle) J. A. Roach and Frank Roberts, (bottom) William L. Logan and E. A. Asman.

Rebecca Moore Mays, 1920s. A native Columbian, Mrs. Mays's husband, Isaac, was train caller and porter at Union Station. She is remembered as an accomplished singer in the First Calvary Baptist Church choir.

The Reverend J. W. Witherspoon (b. 1893), 1920s. Born in Clarendon County, Witherspoon started out as a railway mail clerk and public school teacher and went on to become one of the best-known A.M.E. ministers in the region. He graduated from Allen University in 1922, pastored churches all over South Carolina, as well as in Georgia and Tennessee, and by the early 1930s had become a Presiding Elder. Allen awarded him an honorary doctorate in 1934.

*Opposite:* The Reverend Thomas D. Brown, ca. 1926 to 1928. In early 1926 Father Brown left the Chapel of the Redeemer in Oklahoma City to become rector of St. Luke's Episcopal Church in Columbia. A native of Virginia, he had graduated in 1920 from the Bishop Payne Divinity School in Petersburg. Beverly Roberts remembers that Brown drove a blue Chevrolet touring car and that he operated a store for the benefit of the church in Jaggers Bottom, the area behind Benedict College. Father Brown served St. Luke's until 1928.

St. Luke's Episcopal Church: a group of youngsters and the photographer, 1920s. Roberts was a devout Episcopalian who served as lay reader and junior warden at St. Luke's. The group, shown in front of the St. Luke's sanctuary, has been identified as follows: (first row, left to right) Miriam Roberts, Willie Smith, Henry Perry; (second row) Gerald Roberts, Beverly Roberts, William Perry, Fred Hipp; (third row) Edward Kyer, Robert Perry, Ralph Nelson. Roberts stands at the far right. The Perry boys were children of the rector.

Holy Cross Mission, College Place, Columbia, 1930s. Holy Cross Mission started when the Roberts family went to visit friends in the area one Sunday and Mrs. Roberts was distressed to see children running around in the street, not dressed for the day. The chancel rail in the improvised sanctuary was made from a banister taken from the old post office building when it was being renovated. Roberts is at the far right.

*Opposite:* The Reverend J. C. White, D.D., 1926. Roberts made several portraits of the Reverend Dr. White, who was described as "the man with a cosmopolitan heart and a universal sympathy." White was pastor of Zion Baptist Church during the 1920s and contributed a column to the *Palmetto Leader*. In December 1926 he and the officers at Zion Baptist authorized the use of their church for a mass meeting of those interested in reviving the NAACP in Columbia.

*Opposite:* Unidentified portrait, 1920s.

Unidentified portrait of a woman with a tambourine, 1920s. This woman may have been a song leader in a church, where tambourines were sometimes used in leading the music.

*Opposite:* William M. Atkinson (d. 1938). In his obituary, Mr. Atkinson, a painter by occupation, was referred to as Col. W. M. Atkinson—either because of his high rank in the Knights of Pythias or in honor of his service in the Capital City Guards, a black unit of the state militia that had been established in the late nineteenth century and disbanded in 1902. The uniform he is wearing here resembles that worn by the officers of the Guards.

Unidentified portrait, 1920s.

4-H Extension display, 1920s. This display is believed to have been a part of the Richland County Colored Fair, held annually and organized by County Agent J. E. Dickson, seen here standing at the right. Colored fairs were held in four other counties in South Carolina—Chester, Darlington, Greenville, and Orangeburg—each fall before the State Colored Fair. With Dickson here are Mrs. Marian Baxter Paul (at left), State Home Demonstration Agent, and Mrs. Frances Thomas, Richland County Home Demonstration Agent. In addition to being one of the best-known farm agents in South Carolina, Dickson rose to the highest ranks in Prince Hall Masonic circles.

*Opposite:* Grand Traveling Deputies Cabinet and Grand Ruler of the I.B.P.O.E. of the World, ca. 1925. Those who have been identified here are: (second row, left to right) Alonzo P. Hardy, R. Hopton Paul, G. Lee Ratliff, Dr. E. A. E. Huggins, the Reverend Turner H. Wiseman, Arthur Perrin; (third row) Willis C. Johnson, *unidentified*, Dr. Julian G. Stuart, *unidentified*. Ratliff was state president of the organization at the time.

Dog pulling a signboard, Columbia, 1931. The fight being advertised here was a ten-round feature bout on an all-star boxing-wrestling card at Columbia's Township Auditorium. Allison and Potter were welterweights. Allison won the match. The Aldine Tea Room (seen here at right) was just a few doors west of the Roberts Studio. In the window of the Tea Room is a sign announcing the visit of Negro tenor Roland Hayes, who was scheduled to appear in concert at the Columbia Theatre on 6 February. To the left can be seen the entrance to the Knights of Pythias Hall and signs advertising the offices of dentist Henry D. Harper and realtor J. H. Johnson.

*Opposite:* Unidentified portrait, probably early 1930s.

182

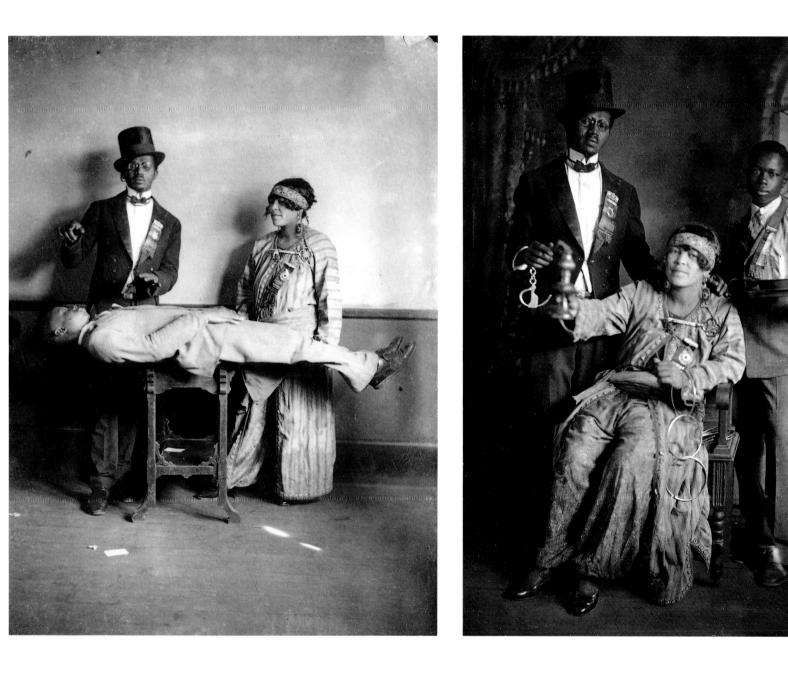

Three photographs of a magician and his assistants, probably 1920s.

Birthday party for Bernice Paul, 1924. Five-year-old Bernice Paul sits elevated in the front row holding a bouquet of flowers. Her father was letter carrier Fabrel Paul, whom Roberts knew well through their membership in St. Luke's Episcopal Church. This picture was taken in front of the Paul home.

Invitation to a birthday party for Miriam Roberts, June 1928. On occasion Roberts created photographic novelties, such as this invitation to a party for his daughter on her eighth birthday. Miriam (1920-1965), the Robertses' youngest child, graduated summa cum laude from St. Augustine's College in Raleigh and became an English teacher, principally at Columbia's C. A. Johnson and Booker T. Washington high schools. She and her husband, Kelly Miller Harvey, Jr., reared three sons. Instrumental in organizing the Richland Association for Retarded Children, she refused to allow it to be established as a segregated chapter and became its first president. She had strong ties with the local chapter of Alpha Kappa Alpha sorority.

A.D. 1928.

I am going to have a birthday party and would like to have you come.

On _MONDAY JUNE 25TH._

At _FOUR:30_ O'Clock

_Miriam A. Roberts_

_1717 Wayne Street._

*Opposite:* Unidentified portrait, 1920s.

The Crusaders Club, State House grounds, 1935. This photograph appeared in the *Palmetto Leader* on 8 August 1935. Seated, left to right, Isaac Brown, Boston Brice, George Kershaw, William Lawson; standing, Jasper Byrd, Jesse Bright, Arthur Cooper, Marion Benton, Henry Thompson, and Albert Williams. The Crusaders was a social club that advocated education and clean living.

Unidentified portrait, 1920s.

The William Cooper Family, Williamsburg County, 1920s. Tobacco farmer William ("Yankee") Cooper owned about a hundred acres in the Jeremiah Community near Hemingway, South Carolina, in Williamsburg County. The Roberts and Cooper families became acquainted through Mrs. Roberts's sister, Mrs. Vivian Gregory Killingsworth, who lived in Florence. One of the Cooper daughters, Hortense, came to live with the Robertses in order to attend Booker T. Washington High School. Pictured here behind Sarah Adele Turner Cooper (seated) are (front row, left to right) Mattie Geneva ("Sing"), Willie Snow ("Bunky"), Sarah Adele ("Seena"), Bertha Josephine ("Buster"), Margaret Cooper (wife of Arthur L. Cooper); (back row) Ruie Park, Mr. William Arthur Cooper, Earley Maple Cooper Donnelly ("Tooter"), baby Ruby Donnelly (Earley's daughter), Hortense Lee. Ruie, an exceptional athlete, was an accomplished boxer.

*Opposite:* Unidentified portrait, probably 1920s.

Men at work, probably 1920s.

Brewer Normal School, Greenwood, 1926: musicians with their instructor. Identified here are Sidney Jackson, from Charleston (third from left), and Miss Geraldine C. Gorum, the music teacher, who had been trained at the Ithaca Conservatory of Music (middle, in front of the piano).

*Opposite: (above)* Brewer Normal School: girls at calisthenics, 1926.

*Opposite: (below)* Brewer students in a domestic arts class. Brewer was founded in 1872 by the American Missionary Society of the Congregational Church and represents a number of small, church-related institutions which sprang up in South Carolina after the Civil War to train blacks as teachers or skilled manual workers. They were funded largely by Northern denominational boards or philanthropists. Brewer prided itself on its able faculty ("from standard institutions") and moderate fees. Enrollment in 1926 was fewer than 200 students. The teacher standing in the middle at the far end of the work counter is believed to be Miss Mattie Malone.

*Opposite:* Bernice Callahan, 1920s.

Louise Gardner Callahan Bing, 1920s. Member of a prominent Allendale family, Louise Gardner married Bernard Callahan, who distinguished himself as a young officer in Europe during World War I, only to die on a Camp Jackson operating table while undergoing a simple appendectomy. She later married C. V. Bing and spent a lifetime in educational work with him in Allendale.

Sara B. Henderson, 1920s. Educated at Cheyney Normal, Hampton Institute, and the University of Pennsylvania, Miss Henderson was a public school teacher in Columbia. But she became most closely identified with "South Carolina's Athens," South Carolina State College at Orangeburg, where she taught for many years. The college's theatrical troupe, the Henderson-Davis Players, was named partly in her honor.

*Opposite:* James E. Prioleau (b. 1906), 1924. Roberts took this photograph of senior James E. Prioleau of Georgetown for the 1925 *Wilkinsonian*, South Carolina State College's first yearbook. After working in New York for a decade as an interior decorator and operator of the Collegian Barber Shop in Harlem, Prioleau returned to Georgetown, serving as teacher and principal in local schools until retirement in 1972. Active in the movement to re-establish participation by blacks in the Democratic primary in South Carolina, he ran for Congress in 1946 as the Progressive Democratic Party candidate from the Sixth Congressional District, losing to the incumbent John L. McMillan. In 1986 he was still barbering in Georgetown and preaching in the Kingstree District of the A.M.E. Church, where he has been a minister since 1962.

Rural church members, probably 1920s.

*Opposite:* Rural church members, probably 1920s.

Richard S. Roberts, probably mid-1930s. The last of several surviving self-portraits of the photographer, this one was probably made near the end of his life. When he died in November 1936, his mother made the trip up from Florida for the funeral and, while viewing the body, remarked without a tear, "Son, you sure wore out; you didn't rust out."

**DATE DUE**

| MAY 5 | 1994 | | |
|-------|------|---|---|
| | | | |
| | | | |
| | | | |
| | | | |
| | | | |
| | | | |
| | | | |
| | | | |
| | | | |
| | | | |
| | | | |
| | | | |
| | | | |
| | | | |
| | | | |

Demco, Inc. 38-293